COLUMBIA COLLEGE CHICAGO

W9-CKT-449

HONORING THE ANCESTORS

JUN 1 9 2009

COLUMBIA COLLEGE LIBRARY
600 S. MICHIGAN AVENUE
CHICAGO, IL 60605

HONORING THE ANCESTORS

James E. Cherry

Progressive Black Publishing Since 1967

Third World Press
Chicago

Third World Press
Publishers since 1967
Chicago

© 2008 by James E. Cherry
All rights reserved. No part of the material protected by this copyright notice may be reproduced, stored in a retrieval system, or transmitted in any form by any means, electronic mechanical, photocopying, recording or otherwise without prior written permission, except in the case of brief quotations embodied in critical articles and reviews. Queries should be addressed to Third World Press, P.O. Box 19730, Chicago, IL 60619.

First Edition
Printed in the United States of America

Cover design and Inside text layout and design by Relana Johnson

Library of Congress Cataloging-in-Publication Data

Cherry, James E.
  Honoring the ancestors / James E. Cherry. — 1st ed.
     p. cm.
  ISBN-13: 978-0-88378-293-4 (pbk. : alk. paper)
  ISBN-10: 0-88378-293-6 (pbk. : alk. paper)
  1. African Americans—Poetry. I. Title.
  PS3603.H484H66 2008
  811'.6—dc22
                          2008014143

12 11 10 09 08   6 5 4 3 2 1

Grateful acknowledgment is made to the editors and publishers of the following publications, where some of the poems in this collection first appeared: *Callaloo, African American Review, Crab Orchard Review, Illuminations, Obsidian, Chattahoochee Review, DrumVoices Revue, Warpland, Bma: Sonia Sanchez Literary Review, Crossroads* and *Black Arts Quarterly*

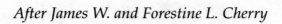

After James W. and Forestine L. Cherry

Contents

contents

Foreword

I was on a bus heading to Salisbury, Maryland when I started reading the poems of James Cherry. Whenever I find myself in Maryland I'm reminded of how southern this state is. I remember reading the slave narrative of Frederick Douglass and reflecting on how he escaped from this part of the country. I read a few of Cherry's poems—paused—then looked out the window of the bus. Cherry's work is deeply rooted in the African American experience and his poems are a roll call of black heroes and their accomplishments. I find the work resonates with me on a spiritual level.

Cherry writes about Emmett Till, Langston Hughes and Paul Robeson. On the bus with me are nothing but blues people. The difference between airplane, train and bus transportation is simply one of class. The poor, the elderly and the college students ride the buses. Here are the dream keepers Langston Hughes wrote about. The poetry of James Cherry is similar and upholds the tradition of black pride and consciousness. The work is also international and one finds Cherry writing about the Nigerian writer and activist Ken Saro Wiwa who was murdered in Nigeria:

> *All you ever wanted is what human beings*
> *the world over want: freedom and dignity.*

In many ways James Cherry in this book is "mapping" a path of remembrance. He is a modern day "literary" abolitionist protecting our ancestors from being abducted a second time. Here are poems to combat historical amnesia and erasure. The African American writer must learn to chart the landscape, read the stars, and know where the river bends. Survival depends on knowledge. Poetry can often be a tool for living. Cherry writes like he has a hammer in his hand.

E. Ethelbert Miller
Director
African American Resource Center
Howard University

Poetry is an echo asking a shadow to dance

—Carl Sandburg

HONORING THE ANCESTORS

The trip from work to the elementary school
is inconvenient and aggravating, trying to fit
a thirty minute drive into an hour lunch break. It
has begun to rain, adding frustration and
treachery to my trek of obligation and duty.

I have determined to cast my vote as an act
of protest against one opponent more so
than an endorsement of the other; a dead man,
would be a more desirable candidate than the
incumbent. Exiting the polling place, the scene
is subdued except for the rhythms of rain tap
dancing over head. I identify myself with photo I.D.
to a middle aged white woman in a yellow blouse who
opens a giant book, her index finger a shovel digging
through its pages to unearth my name from the loam
of other registered voters whose last name begin with C.
I'm passed to a burly balding white man with muscular
hairy forearms who explains to me the virtues
of the process before leaving me to my own devices
and wishing me the best of luck.

The curtain envelops me like a robe, priestly and black
and suddenly, I am not alone, the voting booth crowded
with faces I've seen all my life, whose names I have
never known. They minister to me of water hoses, police
dogs, Alabama bridges, Philadelphia Mississippi, Bull
Connor, Tent City, Sixteenth Street Baptist Church, Emmett
Till, remind me that choosing a candidate is only a vehicle
secondary to the journey itself, a road constructed
of blood, screams, tears, death and not of my own making.
I punch holes in my ballot and plumes of smoke escape
through them, filling the room with an incense in
toxicating and sweet. The hairy forearmed, burly ballot

1

taker checks my card for hints of hanging chads, points
me in the direction of a black woman with gold dangling
earrings who instructs me to sign, tear off the top portion
of my ballot and shove the remainder into a box.

The rain now is relentless coming down in torrents like
the answer to an ancient dance. And it feels good seeping
into the marrow of my bones as I fasten my seatbelt en route
to work like a man returning from a pilgrimage
across arid desert sands halfway around the world.

11/02/2004

FATHER'S DAY 2005

As you lay there, apparition of the man I feared,
family gathered bedside like priests administering
the last rites of silence, Father's Day has brought me
to this Sunday morning fifteen years late.

Over the past months cancer strengthened, encroached
upon lungs and gray matter, devouring memory
of lessons taught in baiting hooks and casting them
with skill and patience, how to keep my eye on the ball, not
always swinging for the fences and that the main thing
was steadying it between the lines no matter which way
road bent or became dirt and loose gravel to where
ever I were going.

The familiarity of my face had become lost
in the hands of hospice workers skilled in syringes
dulled with morphine and obligation.

As with all things, time reduced the virility of thirty
years of factory labor, the dedication for one woman,
the rearing of seven through discipline, encouragement
and bread to the fragility of skin, bone, a breath at a time.
That evening, with eyes rolled heavenward, you smiled
at the rustling of wings overhead and ascended
to grasp at feathers, your life rising in us
carrying forth promises to a generation of flesh
who will one day dare to speak your name.

BIRD REMEMBERED
(for Charlie Parker)

Tommy Dorsey. Now thats some funny shit. Especially
when those jugglers showed up in Baroness' Nica's 5th Avenue
living room in the Stanhope Hotel and you couldnt stop your
self from laughing if you wanted to, not even after you began
to cough, regurgitate and collapse, slipping beyond the grasp
of loneliness, where all things pass away.

You were nobody's down and out junkie. Whiskey and dope
was just easier to come by than compositional theories
on Hindermiths' *Kleine Kammermusik* or meetings with Sartre
in sidewalk cafes over coffee and existential discourses or
the alienation from revolutionizing harmony, rhythm
and tone, having genius mistaken for crazy people music.

You were just tired, cramming 60 years of living into a worn
out 35 year old frame, leaving echoes of courage, sophistication
and virtuosity thundering throughout the background of our
consciousness and a whole bunch of cats, 50 years late, choosing
a freedom you'd embraced a long time ago.

GENEALOGY

There are five generations of Lewis' in the face
of my great great aunt, confined by infirmities
and walls reeking of urine and apathy.

Nellie Murphy is 94 years old and of my mother's people.

A momentary loss of balance resulted in a fractured
hip and now days of rehab have slipped into months
of deterioration and loneliness.
But she still recognizes Forestine's baby boy
and my wife as well, reminiscences about childhood (hers),
weddings (mine), complains about the insipidness of food,
impatience of staff, indifference of family, yearns
to smell the earth of her flower garden, wants the warmth
of her own bed on Cable Ave and elaborates about this
insatiable craving for Sprite and chicken wings.

Sunset finds my wife and I within nursing home walls
sharing wings and soda pop as though it were bread
and wine borrowed from hushed rooms millenniums removed.
And as I hold the glass for her, I notice how frail
she has become with eyes hollow, skin pale and peeling
as if making preparations for another of life's transitions.

Other visitors arrive with Buffalo fish and peach cobbler
as I leave my Aunt Nellie with hugs and promises to return,
soon. Exiting the lobby, our shadows crystallizing in the fall
of twilight, my wife reaches for me, her hand
soft and warm, like something precious,
born only seconds ago.

POSTSCRIPT

Dear Mama,

The last time I said I love you
was six years ago on the seventh floor
in a semi-private room at the county
hospital where you lay shackled by tubes
and machines whose cold indifference mocked
my weary sighs and unrequited moans.

Moments later, you slipped just beyond.

And in the pursuing days, I wrestled with the meaning
of lymphoma, cultivated a growing anger
towards a God omniscient with His or Her
precepts of sin, suffering and death. And since
that time I have filled this space with the compass
of your smile, whispers of words encouraging and
the thought that eternity exists within the speaking
of your name, as I seal this letter within
the folds of my heart, stamped with a kiss
and the letting go.

TRAVELIN'
(for Langston)

With a few jazz albums tucked under
arm, a suitcase in one hand, cigarette
rhythmically bouncing from the corner
of your mouth and the blues . . . you always
carried the blues with you . . . your
footprints are meditating in the sands
of Asia's heat, dancing in the fertile
valley of the Nile delta, marching
triumphantly down the Champs Elysees,
mocking with that smile of yours America
and the ways of white folks.

Words were as natural to you as shaving
three day stubble, lacing a pair of shoes,
doffing your favorite hat, boarding mid
night trains or simply encouraging other
writers who were Black, poor
and trying to find their way.

Because you wrote, wandered and wondered,
I move through space and time to the far
reaches of the earth knowing the brother
hood of man and the omnipotence of a God
who created this lonely planet by molding
breathy words and scattering them
upon the winds of the universe.

ANNIE ALLEN

(for Gwendolyn Brooks)

It was the year of Baraka
and the Black Arts Movement dancing
to the beat of distant drums, chanting
African rhythms of a new love,
language, liberation with raised fists
and even higher consciousness.
And you walked among your people.
And cried, laughed and touched, offering
your home and the cherished position
of sitting at your feet to bathe
in the light of genius, compassion and soul.

Annie Allen is a long way from 1967.

And they grew strong and proud
from the inspiration and insight you hand
fed them, finding wings and voices of their own,
soaring higher places with new songs, but
forever returning home within the shadow
of your neatly cropped afro.
This journey of putting thoughts into words
that I have disembarked upon has been illuminated
by your smile like a beacon calling me
out of the darkness of who I am
and the worlds that encompass me.

EMMETT TILL

(after all these years)

After 50 years, *Bobo, you aint dead yet. You'd be mid
sixties by now gone through that mid life thang, receding
hairline or any hair at all, prosperous paunch from excessive pounds
or the saccharin of success and kids, maybe
even grand kids bouncing upon your knee by now.

Can you believe it? After all these years ever since being
dragged from Uncle Mose's place before daybreak, beaten,
shot, tied to a gin fan and buried in the muddy bosom
of the Tallahatchie, you wont leave these white folk alone,
a ghost hovering over the consciousness of America.

Now, they want to re-open a case with lukewarm leads looking
for accomplices of Bryant and Milam, hoping theyll be black
and that theyll be able to bury you once and for all. You shouldve
kept your ass on that train, enjoyed
the lushness of crops
ready for harvest or cotton fields like small clouds coming outof the
earth or read your favorite book until you fell asleep between its
pages; the Pullman porters would have had your back.
Or better yet, played stickball in the streets of Chicago where fire
hydrants are used to cool the swelter of summer days and it
is no crime to whistle at pretty brown skinned girls or play
a game of hide-and-go-get-it when sunset covers
everything in shadow.

But hey, a northern lynching is the same as a Mississippi one: robes
and hoods exchanged for suits and ties behind institutional walls.
So theres not much difference, about the same length of time between

9

1955 and 2005, a short journey between
pain and remembrance.
I guess it really would not have mattered at all.
Eventually, they would have got you.
It just happened sooner than later.

*Till's nickname

FOR THE LIFE OF POETRY

Today, I went to a poetry workshop instead
of a funeral. No one had heard from my
sister-in-law's sister, forcing family
to break down back doors three days later.

At the workshop, the facilitator (a poet
imitating a college professor) placed pennies
and paper before us to associate images,
memories, thoughts with a copper red cent; I
thought of Tennessee sales tax, penny loafers
and dead presidents.

My sister-in-law's sister, Lillian (such
Southern gentility) was a member of the Faithful
Four, a gospel outfit that had made a reputation
among local congregations and concert goers, who
would now carry on under a spotlight with an
empty space behind a lone microphone where faint
echoes of a soprano once soared, reminding my
sister in law, Delores, that she alone remains
of her mothers' daughters.

But this day the breath of the poet is pregnant
with the word of life, each line breathtaking as
a revelation, phrases sparkling with the light
of truth and images that detonate the universe
into new worlds of promise and immortality.

I fold my guilt and stuff it in my pants, the
exercise feeling like a block of cement
in my back pocket as I limp from the room,
promising to give this poem to Delores on tomorrow
or the next time I saw her, whichever came first.

TOUISSANT

In dank, dark holes of medieval walls on God
forsaken land, imprisoned between French and Swiss
borders, you blow on your hands for heat
but find warmth only in the arms of memory.

The air in the Jura Alps is lucid allowing you to climb
snow capped mountains, turn around, survey vast amounts
of people, plans, places that stretch before your life.

You never wanted war at 50, engineering horse and buggy
into golden sunsets. But slavery wasnt far removed
when the message of the drum echoed, incinerating
the countryside, resurrecting passions forgotten or buried.

You understood that revolution could not subsist upon the milk
of unbridled emotion, but sustenance lay in the marrow
of organization and disciple, beating the white devils
at their own game of playing both sides against the middle.

Genius and greatness are mentioned in the same breath when
ever your name is spoken, teaching half-pint racist French generals
lessons in ass whipping and humiliation, but you
forgot that the devil is the master of deception and the father
of lies when proffering handshakes or discussing
matters of state.

Nightfall: Wrapping tattered blankets around your shoulders,
smiling upon accomplishments and challenges to come, light
at the corners of your mouth like a thousand suns stretch across
waters and eternity into dark crevices wherever freedom
has begun to take root.

BETWEEN FOOTBALL AND FREEDOM

At 17, my nephew runs throws tackles extremely well.
Pimps from prestigious colleges and universities
have solicited his services with perfumed
letters, honey dipped phone calls,
weekend getaways and gifts of extravagance.

Just last weekend, I hugged his 6'2" 215 pound
frame, he beamed, blurted, "Ole Miss."
My mouth hung open from flashbacks of hooded
cowards on horseback brandishing torches
of terror, fat-assed cops with flashing
lights on dark deserted back roads, red
necks and rebels pledging allegiance to con
federate flags snapping in the winds
of white Supremacy and ignorance.

   Say what?
 I can start as a freshman instead of sitting on the bench.
   What about Medgar?
 Theyre in the SEC. To be the best youve got to play the best.
   Philadelphia? Goodman Chaney Schwerner?
 Oxford is a small town.   *Sort of like Jackson.*

Hey man. Youre considered nothing but
a piece of meat wherever you go.
 There are just too many ghosts down there.

My nephew, who has yet to qualify academically
at anyone's school, calmly queried, so whats the
difference between Mississippi and Tennessee?
I looked deeply into his eyes and
saw a reflection of his father, his father's father
and thousands of others, not unlike myself, whose faces
consists of American dreams and broken promises.

Alright man.
Hugging and turning away in goodbye, the fetid
image of a teenage boy fished from muddy waters
rose in my mind like dark foreboding clouds
precariously perched upon the distant horizon.

FROM SUMMER TO FALL

Andre,
man what are you doing?
Its only been 39 summers,
less than that since jr high,
basketball, girls, *Parliament
Funkadelic*, Cumberland and Church
streets where our lives intersected
and entwined for the very first time.
Encroaching manhood brought with it wine,
reefer, college and geographical space
that scattered physically but could
never sever singular moments sewn
into the fabric of time and memory.

Occasionally, our paths crossed at the
grocery store, post office, gas station
and we compared notes on marriage, ex
panding waistlines, 9 to 5's and kids
(you got a boy in high school already?)
and always promised to hook up for beer
and a ball game.

Now, days of procrastination have led
to backrooms of funeral parlors, heavy
with questions like, man what are you doing
here for it is still the month of July
in your life and what were you thinking
in the middle of the night leaving your
final breath upon bathroom floors and did
you, lying here with that frown, some where

between anger and innocence, embrace death
like a new religion or challenge it
like a bandit stealing light
from your sanctuary?

"Peace 'Dre," I toss over my shoulder
and into your open casket while out of doors
I am acutely aware of the colorlessness
of rain, echoes of silence and that I
have grown suddenly cold.

2/13/2001

ROBESON: ARTIST

By the time you suckled upon the breast
of Maria Louisa Bustill, you were already years
ahead of the times you were about to embark
upon, learning lessons of diligence and dignity
with all due perspicacity.

Seventeen years later your brilliance carried you
upon the campus of Rutgers College excelling as Phi
Beta Kappa, debater, lettered athlete, class valedictorian.
After graduation, law degree in hand and working
for a firm where secretaries take no dictation from niggers,
served only to stoke red hot flames of self-expression
searing your bosom, a conflagration of creativity.

The stage called and *Emperor Jones* answered with ballads,
spirituals, arias, folk songs in twenty different tongues
upon Soviet, Asian, European soil, the earth
reverberating from accolade and applause. And from those
wanderings you identified with the suffering of life
regardless of culture and color and being an entertainer
just wasnt enough anymore.

But they didnt understand. They are still with us, those
who refuse to understand that you were artist, a brother
in the family of man who hummed songs of the oppressed
long after the world amputated your legs at the knee,
dissected dreams in your eyes
and surgically removed your tongue.

ROBESON: ACTOR

With a push from Essie, you wandered around
the Village, found yourself upon the doorstep
of the Princeton Players and in the company
of a young playwright anticipating the arrival
of icemen, launching long days journey into night.

Mouths still are agape from the sheer splendor displayed
in *Emperor Jones* and *All God's Chillun Got Wings*, wooing
critics with the eloquence of your power and grace. You
teamed with Lawrence Brown, introduced spirituals into stuffy
concert halls, crying in the wilderness for others to
stand and be counted as Black and artist. First silver
screened under Micheaux, you became disenfranchised
with the Hollywood scene that reinforced stereotypes
of savages and sycophants, save for Song of Freedom.

But for all your thespian triumphs, a stage in London
is where you still live, putting flesh, bone and sinew
upon Shakespeare's words, your strong black hands finding
immortality upon Peggy Ashcroft's slender white neck,
slowly closing around a world wretched and absurd.

ROBESON: ACTIVIST

It ran hot through your veins
on that spring New Jersey morning when
you came kicking and fighting against this world.
Freedom was a rite of passage handed down
from a father absconding North Carolina nightfall,
the north star a calling from God and a mother
whispering lullabies of Quakers practicing
abolitionism in Pennsylvania hillsides.

But it was Britain of the 30s where you discovered
Africa, became acquainted with its sons and daughters,
reveled in the understanding that there is no shame
in being Black, only the power of love and redemption.
Old Man River would never be the same.

Suddenly, the world had grown cold, shivering in the shadows
of nuclear confrontations and you deemed it
unthinkable that Negroes would bear arms for their
oppressors against a land where the only color
of any significance was red.

Standing alone, you told the House Committee on Un
American Activities to kiss your ass, the same way
you would a lynchmob in the outdoors of Peekskill,
realizing the only difference between North and South
was the accent placed upon the word nigger.

Hollywood, Broadway, record companies refused to remember
you name, casting clouds and contemplation of razor blades,
sleeping pills and delusions of walking on air, as you
eternal warrior, penned your own words upon posterity never
regretting your choice to fight for freedom because
it was the only thing you knew how to do.

FIGHT NIGHT

It's Thursday night at the fights on cable tv,
1975 and Muhammad Ali is in Manila with Smokin'
Joe who is trying to separate his head from every
thing else with well-timed left hooks.

My wife, dealing in supper's aftermath,
is in the kitchen with running water, converging silver
ware and the opening and closing of cabinets, shouts
above the commotion into the den, "sweetheart, how
many times are you going to watch that?"

Its early in the fight and the two combatants are going
at it like titans in the final hour of Armageddon fighting
for dominion of the world when the earth was still young.

"It's Muhammad Ali, baby," I reply, comfortable now
in my favorite chair, the tv a pocket watch swinging
before my eyes, the action on the screen mesmerizing
as a hypnotic trance.

I hear her remark about how the same old fight always ends
the same old way no matter how many times I watch it
as she wipes the kitchen table, its surface sparkling clean.

But he will never be old I think to myself, Muhammad
Ali a rare man among men refusing to bear arms
in the name of U.S. imperialism and sacrificing the prime
of his prowess for conviction and consciousness sake. How
can a man grow old who declared "I am the Greatest" uplifting a race
of people relegated to second class citizenship and less

than human status? Forever floating like a butterfly thats
what he will be, elevating a sport to an art form, his
life metaphor for the indomitable human spirit.

They are in the tenth round now and Ali is imposing his
will, closing Frazier's right eye with lightening left jabs
swelling his jaw from the powers majestically invested
in his right fist.

I glance over my shoulder and my wife has broom in hand
scratching the kitchen floor, collecting crumbs into a decrepit
circle. Turning back towards the tv, I shake my head wishing
she would grasp a glimpse of beauty, that she would
recognize what most of the world already knows: that some
things will remain long after all else has passed away.

IMAGES

Even after the preacher mumbled a few dry words: "ashes
to ashes and dust to dust . . ." and they bestowed your body
back to earth, your presence hovers over my shoulder,
timeless sculptures on the shelf of my life.

Chiseled cheekbones, classic lines, eyes deep
set prophetic oracles, the glory of antiquity, the beauty
of shadows, profiles in sculptured ebony where I catch
my own imperfections, shortcomings, possibilities.

I am of the same clay the potter chose.

PORT HARCOURT
(for Ken Saro Wiwa)

For 17 months, you were held with 28 others in governmental
torture chambers on bullshit charges concocted by that bastard
Abacha, his pockets burgeoning with money soaked
in blood and human suffering.

The only thing you were ever guilty of was peace
and ideas. You spoke truth to the Europeans for their
years of environmental genocide against the Niger Delta
and its people, bribing African dictators with gewgaws,
trinkets and baubles stained with profits spewing
from the plush offices so multinational corporations.

The white man is a cruel joke played upon the African continent.

But you were free all along. It was the rest of us on trial. You
had measured your last words like a prophet of locust and wild
honey, walked to the gallows like a natural man, winked
in the direction of the executioner, witnessed the heavens open before
you as your body swayed upon the lifeless air,
like an omen that history was coming to judge us all.

COME THE DAY

(ken saro wiwa)

All you ever wanted is what human beings
the world over want: freedom and dignity.
You never demanded gold, silver or positions
of power, only the right of your people to in
herit the purity of air, water and Nigerian
earth. Your creative gifts were sanctified
to the service of the Ogoni people, like an offering
of the first fruits laid upon the altar
of courage and sacrifice.

You chose to struggle, bleed and cry
within the midst of your people
instead of observing their miseries
behind secluded walls of academia
or across oceans of self-imposed exile. Death
could never intimidate your walk nor extinguish
the magnificence that was your light, shining
more brilliantly than ever, inspiring Black
poets the world over when mere words
become not enough.

A LIFE

(ken saro wiwa)

The age of 13 found you in the halls
of Government College in Umuahia, son
of a businessman and a chief, a long way
from Bori, Rivers State, where all things
European glittered like a dream in distant
moonlight. But from the very beginning
there was never any doubt. Nigerian blood
was always green and white, choosing culture
and community during times of Civil War,
beating frantic rhythms upon ancestor drums
for the Ogoni to fight or be swallowed
by rising tides, rich and black, natural resources
exploited from high rise office buildings
of multi-national corporations.

You built the house of MOSOP, a place
of refuge for 500,000, their struggle for survival
to encompass lifetimes, their futures measured
in 24 hour increments. And for your struggles
to bring atrocities committed against the Ogoni
before the consciousness of the world, you
were charged with a crime, marched
into the Port Harcourt dawn.
A hibiscus blooms where wooden gallows
have long since rotten in the sun.

LUNCH WITH BROTHER

Mike had arranged lunch on a Monday after
noon at a popular deli trendy with the college set
and the buzz of business deals of men with well
trimmed beards in blue suits and red neckties.

He is my older brother and has been thinking
about words and their correlation to his life,
desiring to document his rise into entrepreneurship,
now wearing success like a three piece Italian suit.
Not very long ago home for him was the helplessness
of public housing, but today its gated communities
on the other side of town, real estate reserved
for athletes, doctors, bankers.

I order a reuben on rye; he settles for a salad, words
not being the only thing on his mind. Idle chatter
solidifies into outlines, titles, structure, chapters,
publishers and I see the answered prayers of my mother
from the light in his eyes and my father's determination
in profile the way Mike cocks his head at an angle
when I advise on copyrights, agents and editors.

Conversation dissipates into politics, sports, mutual
funds, a half-eaten reuben (eyesight more voracious
than appetite) and chocolate ice cream for desert.
Outside, we exchange comments on the weather and
promises to sit down with tape recorders for the sake
of posterity before we embrace and shake hands, a
generation of dreams converging in the space
where our flesh presses together.

DRIVIN' NIKKI

I'm in Nashville after a two-hour drive
to chauffeur the poet down I-40 to be feted by
the local library before a read at a local Black College.
She emerges from the airport concourse like royalty in
black pin stripes with matching tie. She is
preoccupied with thought (probably constructing
poems, editing essays, grading students' papers), head
bowed, bag over one shoulder, another in her arms
with a neatly cropped black and silver Afro glowing
angelically above her head as I approach with extended
arms of welcome and respect.

The drive is fueled with banter of Tupac, jazz, Iraq,
writers (dead, living) until halfway home I pop in Duke's
Jazz Party and we fall silent, save for Nikki tapping her
feet, erupting in joy whenever Jimmy Rushing got good,
laughter sanctified and pure. I sneak sideward glances
in her direction as she reads linear notes, looking for signs
of apathy that come with tenured professorship, victories
with bouts of cancer and plaudits hung upon celebrated
writers. But I only see fire, the same fire she sparked
over thirty years ago with *Nigger Can You Kill* that raged
against the consciousness of a young Black man trying to find
himself and definitions of America and what either
of them had to do with tomorrow. I want to tell her that she
is one of the reasons I write . . . but we are inside the city's
limits and stop for barbecue ribs and sweet tea instead.
I buy lunch for Nikki Giovanni.

Later, in the auditorium, she hypnotizes the audience
with wit, insight, intelligence and closes the evening
by dedicating a poem to me from her latest release, *Quilting
the Black Eyed Pea*. Afterwards, I want to really tell her
how much her words have impacted my life but she is swarmed

by fans, well-wishers and admirers and only our eyes are able
to speak. I pump my fist against the air in her direction;
she nods as though she has known all along that sometimes
some words are better understood when not spoken at all.

BAPTISM

The preacher raises his hand, stirring a hush
that rises above the congregation in moans, patted
feet and spirituals designed of slaves throwing
off the scent of paddy rollers and hounds.

Two girls await the wings of baptism. They
are 13 and 14, barefoot, black skin contrasting
the purity of robes, smile nervously, fidget,
communicate with one another through the language
of nods and glances, silent tongues
only siblings understand. Wading into water,
they declare names, profess Jesus is Lord
and that they are ready to apply death to flesh.

Afterwards, there are hand claps of praise, shouts
of song and the joy of new life as two souls
emerge onto slippery footing, the water serene
as a borrowed tomb on a bright Sunday morning.

AWAKENINGS
(for Sonia)

At nine years of age, Harlem
mustve seemed like another planet when you arrived.
Alabama mud on your shoes, your hand securely
in the hand of a father who drummed polyrhythms
to make ends meet.

Four years of Hunter after high school and Louise Bogan's
creative writing class followed that. But after a year, you
had answered your calling, had little use for the stuffy
halls of academia.

You bought into King's vision of white kids and black
kids on integrated playgrounds and even became a card
carrying member of the Congress for Racial Equality, until
you met an ex-hustler in a bow tie outside a coffeehouse
who used a soapbox for a pulpit preaching black is
beautiful, self-determination and that the white
man is the devil.

It was the first day of the revolution.

Young and artist, black and political, you gathered
handfuls of invective and hurled them at a cruel system, white
and unjust, you were Nzingha reincarnate, our warrior princess,
pithy, passionate, profane, but always beautiful.

WILSONIA BENITA DRIVER
(1934, Sonia)

In the name of your father
you were welcomed with adoring arms
into an Alabama September, shortly thereafter
there was only Pat, Dad and the omniscience of God.
But Grandmama, with her unconditional hugs
and succulent kisses, mended circles once broken
beyond repair, until God anointed her with wings
without your consent, and the world became a big, cold,
lonely place for a little girl barely six years of the age.

But each night, after you'd crawled into bed, blankets
tight around your shoulders, you began to hug words
like a favorite teddy bear before falling into sleep, knowing
Grandmama was as close as a mumbled prayer or moonlight
falling through your window, soft and warm.

YOU A BaddDDD SISTAH

Sistah, you aint never took no stuff off nobody, not
even Etheridge when he was shooting that shit leaving
you with kids to raise and your own way to make
as best a Black woman could.

Afterwards, when you got into Malcolm (or did Malcolm
get into you) you couldnt accept the Nation's second
class status relegated for women. And even down
in the Village, where you work shopped with Lil' Leroy,
Don L Lee and Larry Neal, the godfathers of BAM, they
couldnt push you around with misogynistic attitudes of the day.

The Bronx Was Next. But you never stopped believing
in the redemptive power of love between a Black man and woman.

Your artistic longevity has made crooked paths straight
and a lot freer to travel for poets who honor your greatness,
continually guided by your spirit along the way.

BEGINNINGS

(August 21 1791, Haiti)

In the heat of Bois Caiman, night shimmered
around circles of dance, perspiring the spirit of Petwo, Dutty
Boukman exhorting worshipers with words African and ancient.

Rum stained parched lips, the rhythm of the drum intensifying
like the pulse of a fever until the moon waxed full
like a revelation over Caribbean sky.

Ogun spoke through the voice of a woman prophesying
of Boukman, Jean-Francois, Biassou, Jeannot
and fields white with harvest.

The squeals of a pig were silenced at the point of a blade
sliding over its throat, blood flowing fast, rich and black
like a tomorrow long overdue.

TO LANGSTON

Brother,
you forever had your ear bent to the pave
ment of Lenox Avenue and 124th Street, listening
for the approaching hoofbeats of Black culture.
You with pen and paper in hand, recorded cadences,
tones, rhythms, mannerisms of a people you deemed
graceful and called your own.

Eschewing ivory towers and even whiter patrons,
you were the people's poet holding up a re
flection of words for them to see the beauty
of themselves. And the ugly too. You felt the pain
of struggle because you were weary too, under
stood the blues because you were born Black
in America, dug jazz knowing life and freedom are
inseparable, appreciated the ingenuity of our
selves and the simplicity of laughter, shed
tears that mingled with a river flowing of Black
frustration, disappointment and pain.

Brother,
in whatever corner of the globe that you found
yourself ensconced, you memorized echoes of Harlem
and scribbled them upon the face of the planet
promulgating, exhorting, celebrating
to the universe and worlds beyond the worth,
dignity, uniqueness, love, soul of a people
that magnificently were, will eternally be
and gloriously remain.

RESURRECTION

I was born between the mildewed pages of *Native
Son* and *Invisible Man*. Through the blood and
screams of thought, I came kicking into a world
hostile and mute, embraced meaning and consciousness
in the outstretched arms of light.
At the breast of Camus and Dostoevsky I suckled
upon milk of existentialism; Hemingway and Steinbeck
encouraged me to stand and walk paths of my own.

I sat at the feet of Countee Cullen and Langston Hughes
learning dance to rhythms ancient and sweet.
Salinger and Hesse rounded off the black and white edges
of adolescence with understanding and color.
Brother Malcolm and Jimmy Baldwin
taught me how to articulate this anger growing
in frustration until devotion displaced
disillusionment, discipline self-destruction.

I have known lovers who have seduced the night
into orgasmic fury and I have sighed their names
on the face of morning: Katharine Anne Porter, Alice Walker,
Sylvia Plath. Eudora Welty, Zora Neale Hurston, Flannery
O'Conner are surrogate mothers who have kissed
my bruised ego scraped upon rejection letters in self
addressed stamped envelopes. Faulkner
continues to live right next door.

Words are my third day rising, breath feeding the brain,
rivers overflowing veins, clay beneath my fingernails
from where I've tried to build monuments to the dignity
of man and bridges across the interminable sky,
like a prayer upon the altar of God.

SYMPATHY FOR SADDAM

Man, you didnt have a damn thing
to do with 9/11. Matter of fact, when they pulled
you from that hole, unshaven, dirty for days,
paraded before the world's eye, prodded
and poked you like something created in the laboratories
of Washington DC, you didnt want a damn thing
to do with nothing.

You had become comfortable making your bed
of earth's floor, breaking bread with rodents and engaging
in philosophical debates with the sound of your own
voice. All you wanted is what all presidents the
world over want: the right to be left the hell alone. You
are a bastard of bastards, gassing the Kurds, (chemicals
from US stockpiles), torturing the Shiites, pillaging
the country's coffers. But there are no WMDs
or sleeping with Osama only black gold and unlike Texas
oil, cheap and plentiful, and you expendable like an unspent
shell casing after a ten year border battle with the Ayatollah.

So, this Sunday morning, they gotcha shackled to a cage,
ripping out your fingernails with food, sleep and sensory
depravation as the Tigris and Euphrates are parceled out
to capitalist pigs and the future of the Iraqi people a mere
footnote in the annals of Western Civilization.

12/14/2003

LOWER NINTH WARD

Its been three days, maybe four, since
the world began to pass me by.
Brackish water come to reclaim what
was rightfully hers. Occasionally, a
swollen body is caught in the ebb and
flow, lodged between parked cars.

I punched holes in the attic and climbed
through them barefoot, blue jeans, t-shirt.
Without money or transportation, there
was nowhere else to go.

The world looks unreal from here: people
and places that defined parameters
of my life forever gone. And it feels
as though I've been here before, suspended
between a prayer and tumultuous sky waiting
to be rescued by a government of constitutional
amendments, reconstruction, forty acres, mules.

As a solitude of stars hovers over roof
tops there is comfort in the hush they bring,
songs without words that rise in my throat
like moans to keep fear and death at bay.

LONG WAYS FROM HOME

They said this was going to be the big one,
the one to wipe the city off the face of the map.
We got word early that morning and started our
march, the Superdome looming on the horizon
like a ship at waters' edge. There was all
kinds of people, ten thousand people, who had
watched their kids drown or had loved ones
unaccounted for but mostly poor and black people
like me with bags, blankets and bundles.

And at first we thought everything was gonna be
alright and it was until Monday when the power
went out and toilets backed up and trash cans over
flowed and there was no food or water or medicine
until smoke started to fill the arena and there
was no air to breathe at all.

All that time rumors were rampant of gangs
with guns and girls being raped and people robbed
and other people sick and dying in darken corners
and the police promising that buses were coming,
coming, coming leaving behind a culture and
community in ruins half a country away.

So, weeks later, I'm telling my story, writing this
a stranger on bitter earth in a dubious new world.
For three days in September I fashioned light
from the bowels of hell. Nothing can hurt me now.
Not even Salt Lake City.

OBJECT LESSONS

By the time wind and rain unleashed its fury
upon the neglect of man made levees, I
had become well learned in lessons of survival.

They were instincts first developed in the holes
of ships lying in feces and vomit chopping Atlantic
waters towards strange new worlds, rehearsed
in fields of southern plantations regurgitating new
songs in foreign tongues, worshiping gods
in images of slave masters, dreaming of a land just
beyond the river, skills honed in days of Jim Crow,
delivered hat in hand or from the shadow of smiles.

Three days later there was food and medicine
rotting on grocery shelves, rafts constructed
of imagination and the clothes on my back
migrating towards the city's horizon
where tomorrow resembled a rainbow,
dauntless and bright.

PRETTY WHITE GIRLS

(for emmett till)

Peeking over the horizon of day,
I see the brilliance of new light
tangled in the blonde sunrise
of your sleeping hair.
Your skin pulsating from the morning
chill, draws you to me like a silk magnet.
I count each pore and follow lines
Into curves and curves atop pink-capped mountains,
probing down warm hirsute valleys.

In the corners of your yawning eyes, blue
mirrors reflect faceless men, drinking
bitter waters of muddy rivers, eating
red white and blue flames, vomiting
God on the crucified air.
I turn quickly, thinking
I've heard the call of a 14-year-old boy, but
it is only the voice of the wind
as I squeeze my genitals
and feel nothing.

BEAT

(bob kaufman)

Kerouac ordered toast and coffee. Black.
When he finished, you tossed your apron
upon the floor of the LA Hilton, walked out
of its doors, northward, giving no one a two
weeks notice; Jack didnt even leave a tip.

Feet calloused, broke and hungry, you feasted
on the poetry, music, dance, art of a North
beach community overflowing with thought
and freedom, a renaissance of love and flowers.

Carrying your son Parker around like a bebop
tune into coffeehouses, you bumped into Ginsberg
and Corso, while breathing your poems, the air
thick with surrealism, palpitating with change.

While others protested the war by burning govern
ment cards, clashing with the gestapo or fleeing
for borders, you detonated *Abomunist Manifestos*,
threw silence like a molotov cocktail. John F
Kennedy had long since left Dallas by then.

Ten years later it was over, our troops battered,
broken and beaten had returned to thankless,
inimical soil as you sat in the San Francisco Bay
looking at the horizon where the world ends,
anxiously anticipating all of those ships
that never sailed to appear over the ocean's edge.

MIGRATION SERIES

(for Jacob Lawrence, Panel 1)

It could have been Goree with clearly
marked points of destination, a mass
of huddled Blackness in the tatters
of winter apparel dragging suitcases
of Southern possessions, the sum
of American dreams, as movement
queues through century old portals
into the crowded silence of whiteness
falling off the edge of the world, faint
sounds of hope echoing near the bottom.

GUEVARA: BEGINNINGS

The eldest of a construction engineer, you had
all the advantages any kid could ask for. And even
for the sake of failing health, your family sacrificed
the comfort of Rosario for the drier climate
of Alta Gracia Cordoba, where you learned reading
and writing at the feet of your mother, excavated
your father's library unearthing treasures of Freud and Marx.

Age 20 had taken you to university studies in Buenos
Aires devoting time and energies to maladies of the skin
and there became initiated into circles of the underprivileged,
beggars at the altar of need.

And in between studies you and Albeto witnessed many
things from the your bike speeding along the coast
of Argentina, through the Andes into Chile, later north
ward to Peru, Columbia and Venezuela, came to under
stand that if one human being was exploited, abused,
dispossessed then you were a lesser man for it.

You never looked back, racing against the wind with your ear
bent for the faintest hue and cry of suffering
down a road paved with triumphs, impassable
with disappointments, always never ending
with the promises of tomorrow.

GUEVARA: HEY YOU

They had you on the run in the middle of 1954, CIA
operatives with Guatemalan blood on their hands and
a hit list of individuals marked for elimination, torture
and deportation in their back pockets. You and Hilda
would split shortly thereafter.

Mexico City was a place of refuge and destiny, your
humanity crossing the ideals of a Cuban revolutionary
in self-imposed exile found guilty of delivering a stillborn
coup d'etat at the doorstep of the presidential palace.

However, by the tender hours of that first meeting you
had pledged the Hippocratic oath to the service of the
26th of July Movement, eventually trading
medicine for machine guns.

But Batista's boys were too strong on that December
morning on the coast of Oriente, forcing you, Raul and
Fidel into the Sierra Maestra to wax strong in strategy,
brotherhood and the movement of shadows.

Three years later, Batista fled and took with him
On a New Year morning U.S. imperialism, corporate
corruption and years of human suffering as you stepped
from the side of that mountain, long haired with red beret
at a rakish angle, to thunderous applause reverberating
from Africa to Asia, Argentina to Alabama and across
deserts of oppression and wastelands of misery or any
place upon the face of the earth where man
thirsts for a solitary drop of freedom.

GUEVARA: FINAL HOURS

The air must have been thin and in short supply near
Vallegrande amongst mountain lushness surrounded
by 1800 Bolivian troops skilled with U.S. weaponry,
well versed in CIA mendacity.

You were only a band of 50, abandoned by the locals,
denied reinforcements from Havana, running low
on supplies, moral, time until shackled and bleeding, marched
across Latin American landscapes, 30 kilometers to La
Higuera into guarded houses of learning.

Thirty-nine year of resistance, struggle and revolution
had all come down to this: one moment of squared
shoulders, head held high, final words of myth and legend,
bullets ripping through flesh and you finding an absolute
freedom, pure and exhilarating, like a long sigh
into a pink dawn where all things are new and eternal.

BLACK SMOKE

(the election of a pope)

There is smoke over the Vatican
this day, black smoke. The same smoke that hung
like blessings over ships embarking
from European ports of call, sailing
gloriously to gather cargoes from west
ward shores. Same black smoke wafting
over the diaspora for centuries to come
with connotations of all things ignorant,
unclean and evil. Smoke . . . bitter
thick, acrid black smoke repugnant
in the nostrils of God, stinging the eye of history,
lingering long after earth is a solitary ember.

DESSALINES

You scooped Touissant's last dream from the filth
of prison floors and breathed fire into it.
"War for war, crime for crime, atrocity for atrocity,"
sharpened the point of your sword the way blood
dripped from the mouths of Leclerc and Rochambeau,
devouring women and children simply because
they were poor, black and dreamed of tomorrow.
There was only one solution: everything white
had to die that freedom may be delivered.
The national flag has only two colors now.

On a cold November, the Haitian morning was rewarded
with surrender and sunrise, your righteousness causing
the Western world to tremble, white slave holders
in fear of drum and shadows.

FLIGHT
(Haiku)

Squinting in sunlight
Brought up for fresh air and dance
Spreads her wings and flies

HOMECOMING

(for Gil Scott-Heron)

It must have began those many Southern
summers ago, walking the gauntlet of grotesque
curses spat from thin twisted mouths
of Klansmen without sheets.
You were 12 years old, one of three frail
Black children and Tigrett Jr. High must have
seemed like a nebulous ideal lost between fear
and *Brown v. the Board of Education.*

Shortly afterwards, you packed your dreams
in maternal bags and migrated to manhood
in colder climates with mountains of stone and steel.
The truth of poetry discovered you somewhere
between then and now as we patted our feet
to your syncopated rhythms, hipping us to Johannesburg,
a place as distant as it was familiar, that
revolutions have no sixty second breaks and
that seasons had forever changed in America.

Recently, news from New York has saddened me
about the changes youre going through, but I just wanted
this message to reach you the way youve reached
me through the profundity of your utterances, praying
that youll find redemption in your next lyric
as the stage lights flash from red to blue and you
like some gray-haired prophet returned from exiled
islands adorned in faded blue jeans carrying
an African beat and a microphone as if
they were the last chapters of the final word
from the Book of God.

RUNAWAY SLAVE

(Haiku)

Red moonless midnight
Yapping hounds sniffing death air . . .
Freedom on my mind

AMADOU

Each night, as I step beyond the four
walls of my apartment, the wind awaits
and wails like a mother delivering her
child to auction blocks on Southern courthouse steps.
Your name has become a cry falling
upon stone ears of justice, who remains
unbalanced and unyielding in deferred
silence and truth.

The world heard the New York night ex
plode into 41 pieces of bone and bullet,
splintering dreams and family bonds over
oceanic tides, your spirit caught up
with those of the ancestors, leaving
bruised flesh crumbled on vestibule floors,
its carpet insatiable like a sponge.

Now what will halt the anger of demanding
feet, who shall wipe away pain streaking
our cheeks, where will our screams go
that become entangled among the clouds, when
will the constitution no longer be antiquated
words on mildewed paper, how am I to sing
America's song when lamentations are
lodged within my throat?
I must move on. The sun has fallen
into the earth. I have become a mere shadow,
standing here my wallet is way too black.
And with each step I take, the wind howls,
Amadou Amadou,
Amadou.

2/27/2000

51

COAL MINER SONG

Like my daddy and his daddy before him,
I harvest black diamonds at the navel
of the earth. This is what I do. There was not
much else to do at age 15, high school drop
out, married, infant mouths to feed.

Three times a week, lunch pail and hard
hat in tow, I outdo Jesus Christ: it took Him
three days to raise from the dead; I'm buried
and resurrected every 13 hours. I don't mean
that in no bad way, especially since my life
is in His hands, Him and the International Coal Group.
Wintertime is worst. Not the dirt and grime,
but the air that dries the mines and creates more
dust which eventually will catch fire
from a smaller explosion and cause a bigger one
and then everybody is blown to hell. If that don't
get you *black damp* will when the explosion
burns up all the oxygen and you're breathing whats
left of your SCSR and when that runs out hope
fully you'll see loved ones on the other side.

I think about that sometimes when I'm putting
my boots on in the early morning darkness, but
once I kiss my wife and am out the door there
are bills to pay, clothes for kids, a roof in need
of repair and its another day riding the cart
patting my foot to the metallic music it makes
coming out of the dog hole the same way I went in.

LAST TESTAMENT
(Sago Miners)

Forty hours after the world ended, there remains
thirteen of us 13000 feet in the bowels of darkness
where the earth moves like the pulse of God. We
find safe haven in remembrance sharing breaths
of air as if it is unleavened bread passed around our
circle, leaving throats parched and longing for wine.

Glancing at the youngest among us, he reminds me
of myself at that age, idealistic and afraid, hope
still flickering in the light of his eyes. But there
is only the fading whine of drills and the curses
of man overhead now, these words written as best I
know how and a desire for warmth and comfort
in the bosom of sleep. Just sleep.

INMATE 29300
(Tookie)

Even after they strapped you to that gurney
at one minute past midnight, you remained un
broken, an indictment against the justice system,
blood in the eye of America.

You were the centuries old *bad nigger* born
fifty-one one years ago where there was no little league
baseball, Boys and Girls clubs or Big Brothers
to pull your coat, found love only on street
corners, in the embrace of colors.

There was no need for final statements, Nobel
nominations had said it all. How many times do
you have to deny 1979, shotguns, four dead?
Besides, Barbara was there.

For twelve minutes the government perfected
techniques in torture, seeking veins for sodium
pentothal until there would be no more inner demons
to wrestle, blown kisses from supporters, pilgrimages
toward redemption or seeking salvation in sanctuaries
built by the hands of man.

MIGRATION
(Haiku)

Blazing cotton fields
Exchanged for frigid train rides . . .
Tears in the city

WORDS OF A POET
(Li-Young Lee)

Whether upon the page or behind podiums, words
unspoken resonate with clarity and potency. Between
each syllable and phrase sacredness is a burnt
offering sweet in the nostrils of God. The symbolism
of space is metaphor, color, tone, simile to your art,
acknowledging something greater than what we have
become. This night, the audience stands and applauds
what has been said, throws palms of praise at your feet;
I kneel in the remaining solitude and begin the pray.

GUN

I am the cold blue steel of the American dream,
cloaked in articles of the Constitution, deified
by those who kill for the glory of sport.

I was in the backpack of your son
when he entered Mrs. Watson's English class,
tired and lonely.

I was hiding beneath socks, underwear
when your daughter could take no more drunken
footfalls through the door.

I was solace for you husband at day's end
after the company moved, leaving no
forwarding address.

I was on street corners when Black boys decided
to value $100 sneakers more than the image
of God.

I was aimed between the eyes of Joe the grocer
as he stood behind the counter reaching
for weapons of his own.

I was pointed with precision towards the balcony
of the Lorraine Motel on an April morning
when there would be no more dreams.

I am the erection stroked, kissed, made love
to. There are no prophylactics.

AN OPEN LETTER TO CLAUDE WILKINSON

I've never seen words sparkle with such technical
brilliance, the way they do when assembled upon
your page. You are a master craftsman building, re
building the consciousness of our lives, metaphor,
simile, assonance, dissonance well-honed tools
of your trade. And even with brush and easel, your
precision coruscates from the canvas like a precious
stone bathed in shadow and light.

But when did you forget that you were a black man
Mississippi born, Southern bred, an American
survivor? Exercising angst is part and parcel of every
poet's repertoire, a standard chosen from the song
book of human experience. But where is the outrage
in your craft at the racial degradation heaped upon your
people 400 years counting, the concern for social justice
in the time of war and the exasperation of a culture
prostituted upon the altar of the dollar almighty?

What made you think you could seclude yourself
Behind walls of ivory towers or seek refuge just across
the Tennessee line and speak only of snails, skinny
dipping or traversing through woods? Leave that to the white
boys who are adept at putting pretty words on paper.
They havent had anything to say in years anyway.

Just ask the masters, Wilk: Dostoevsky will tell you that it
was Russian culture that birthed *Crime and Punishment*,

Malamud would testify that *The Fixer* sprang from Jewish
soil, Shakespeare will remind you that he never gave stage
directions from China, Mexico or India and listen, as others
are encouraging you to pour libations in the land of your
ancestors, that there is no shame in being Black and poet.

BLACKMAN ON TRIAL

I've been sitting
in America's courtroom
for the last 400 years, sitting
before the Great White Father
in his robes of Black, feeling
the sting of his red white and
blue gavel crashing down
upon my skull.

Handcuffed to the illusion
of the American dream, shackled
by broken promises of what
I could have become, I've
been in a holding cell
of solitary disenfranchisement subsisting
off of the stale bread of freedom
and the sour tears of my ancestors
that nourished the land.

Now, I stand before the jury
of the world, accused of being
a welfare recipient gangbanger rapper
drugdealer athlete genetically
inferior rapist murderer buffoon sex
maniac, a natural born suspect.

I stand accused of being three
fifths a man, a nigger, a non-human
being, as court is adjourned
and just above the judge's head, outside
the window, the hangman's noose dangles
from a stolid venerable tree.

My steps are measured, proud
and righteous, as armed guards
with bayonets in my back,
lead me from the scene.

SISTER BETTY

In quietness and strength,
you supported and encouraged an ex
hustler in his rise beyond the ranks
of Black nationalism to the cause
of human dignity, helped him shoulder
his burden unto the doorsteps of the world.

In quietness and strength,
you watched hired assassins take cover under
the Audubon Ballroom, aim and fire with words
Assalam Alaikum bleeding from his mouth
upon your lap, leaving a kingdom
without a prince.

In quietness and strength,
you taught, raised, nurtured six in the line
of Shabazz about culture, dignity and love
exhorting them from the nest to fly as hard,
as high and wide as human wings and dreams
could carry, admonishing responsibility
with freedom.

In quietness and strength,
you rubbed your head against college walls
throwing caps and gowns in the air, stepping
inches taller, chin chiseled in pride, ascending
to levels of prestige, position and titles:
Dr. Betty.

In quietness and strength,
you stood cold and forlorned but not forgotten
in the shadow of widows from Camelot
and mountaintop dreams, but you lived in no
ivory towers and chose to embrace us
in the affection of your touch.

In quietness and strength,
you clothed, housed and fed your husband's
namesake, then fought his demons with every
thing that was within you the way you had been
fighting all your life, until nothing was left
but smoke, ashes and whispered words upon your lips:
"take care of little Malcolm."

You won Sister Betty.
You breathe Sister Betty.
You live Sister Betty.

In quietness and strength,
take your rest.

QUESTION
(for Haitian refugees)

What made you think you could sail westward
winds in makeshift boats overcrowded with hunger
and hope, ease your children down into the cold
blue waters off freedom's shore, its sands
sparkling like jewels of opportunity, mistake
Miami for the beaches of Normandy, pile into pick
ups fueled by capitalistic dreams dashing down
interstate highways trying to outdistance poverty,
death and history, only to be cattle prodded into
barbed wired camps more squalid than native soil?

What made you think that you were Irish, German
or Cuban, that this was land for tired huddled masses,
that you were not poor and black and politically expendable?

10/2002

A REVOLUTIONARY'S DILEMMA

When I think about all that my people
(Black people. I cant speak for anyone else)
have endured, overcome between the oceans
of this land: chattel property, black codes,
lynching, disenfranchisement, helplessness, etc.,
the rise or decline of America wouldnt bother
me one way or the other.

But three hundred and sixty five days later,
listening to the more than 3000 names
resurrected from the rubble of spiraling
monuments, five sided buildings and open fields
become hallowed ground, I dont know what to feel.

The faces (White people. The media has conveniently
forgotten its Black victims) flashed on the evening
news are hallow and hopeless humanity trying to fill
holes in their lives with photos and memorabilia
of loved ones, the way I would be doing also if my flesh
did not return at the end of the day . . . I
understand more clearly than ever that I am America
whether I want to be or not and that America is me.

The day has been one long memorial to grief
and remembrance, wearying mind and body.
But one thing is for certain: I aint
waving no goddamn flags for nobody.

09/11/2002

About The Author

James E. Cherry is the author of *Shadow of Light*, a novel published in the U.K. by Profile Books in 2007 and scheduled for release in the U.S. in June 2008. His poetry has been featured in journals and anthologies both nationally and internationally. An educator and social critic, he resides in Tennessee with his wife Tammy.

For more information visit www.jamescherry.com

Special thanks to Gwendolyn A. Mitchell, my editor, for her insight and encouragement.